# KUMUKANDA

# KUMUKANDA

## Kayo Chingonyi

Chatto & Windus
LONDON

3 5 7 9 10 8 6 4 2

Chatto & Windus, an imprint of Vintage,
20 Vauxhall Bridge Road,
London SW1V 2SA

Chatto & Windus is part of the Penguin Random House
group of companies whose addresses can be found at
global.penguinrandomhouse.com

First published by Chatto and Windus in 2017

penguin.co.uk/vintage

A CIP catalogue record for this book is
available from the British Library

ISBN 9781784741396

Typeset in India by Thomson Digital Pvt Ltd, Noida, Delhi
Printed and bound in Great Britain by Clays Ltd, St Ives plc

Penguin Random House is committed to a sustainable future
for our business, our readers and our planet. This book is made
from Forest Stewardship Council® certified paper.

*I.M. Thomas Kareem Crosbie, aka PACE, 1988–2016*

# Contents

# Author's Note

Meaning 'initiation', *kumukanda* is a ritual that marks the passage into adulthood of Luvale, Chokwe, Luchazi and Mbunda boys, from North Western Zambia and its surrounding regions. As part of these rites, young boys live separately from their community in a bush camp, where they are taught skills that will aid them in a productive life. *Makishi*, a festival of dance, song and theatrical performance, marks the return of the initiated as men. Throughout *kumukanda* and *makishi*, masks represent communion with the spirits and teach important lessons about the history of the tribe. This book approximates such rites of passage in the absence of my original culture.

# KUMUKANDA

# The Colour of James Brown's Scream

*for Steve McCarthy and Todd Bracey*

I have known you by many names
but today you are Larry Levan,
your hand on the platter in the smoky
room of a *Garage* regular's memory.
You are keeping 'When Doves Cry'
in time, as you swing your hips,
and sweat drips from your hair
the colour of James Brown's scream.
*King of King Street*, we are still moving
to the same sound, though some
of us don't know it is your grave
we dance on, cutting shapes
machismo lost to the beat –
every road man is a sweetboy
if the DJ plays 'Heartbroken'
at just the right time for these jaded feet.
Teach us to shape-shift, Legba,
you must know I'd know your customary
shuffle, that phantom limp, anywhere;
that I see your hand in the abandon
of a couple, middle of the floor,
sliding quick and slick as a skin-fade
by the hand of a Puerto Rican clipper-man
who wields a cutthroat like a paintbrush.
Let us become like them, an ode
to night, ordering beer in a corporeal
language from a barman who replies
by sweeping his arms in an arc,
Willi Ninja style, to fix a drink our lips
will yearn for, a taste we've been
trying to recreate ever since.

# Self-Portrait as a Garage Emcee

### I.

117 Retford Road, Harold Hill, Essex.
I can't sleep because there are no sirens,
no neighbour's screams lulling me
to lurid dreams of Natasha Laurent.
There is no panoramic view for solace
but in the right light this window
shows, not this white-flight-satellite-town,
but south London from seventeen floors up:

the River Wandle a coiled snake
swallowed by the Thames,
friends crossing the road
to the park in my absence,
the alley between flats where Sacha blasts
a tattered ball into the goal-net simulacrum,
a wall against which his brother Stacey stands,
hands shrouded in Goalie Gloves.

It is our first night in this grieving house.
I miss listening to Delight 103.0
and with no tapes to remind me
the best bet is Kiss 100 but they don't play the songs
for which my cheap headphones exist.
When we pitched up the neighbours spoke of how
*the old girl, God rest her soul, wasn't found for days*
and, though the family tidied up for a quick sale,
there was a staleness when we prised the door open,
its hinges stiff, wood swollen in the late summer heat.

*

If you were to walk the four and a half miles to Crow Lane
you'd see her name in their one stone, she *fell asleep*
three years after him and they're *dearly loved, sorely missed*
but no less gone for that. When all is quiet I can still hear
the sirens through gaps in the barred windows,
still see the power station dusky and unused in a distance
that seems to stretch to the edge of everything. The smog
in which garage music lives and everybody's got lyrics.
I can still hear Peter Biggs saying:

> *Enter with the Eastender*
> *Peggy with the breast cancer*
> *Tiffany try make baby*
> *Mark with the HIV*

In Harold Hill the girls ask if I'm from *up London*,
smile when I nod like we've come to some understanding.
Sensing I *have a voice* Mr Cox tries to make me join
the swing band, I say no. I end up singing 'Living La Vida Loca',
in midnight blue shades, anyway. For months the hours
before mum comes home pass in the wake of drive-time pop.
Until flicking through stations, one dark afternoon,
I hear those click-and-clack-hi-hats and stop on Majik FM.

II.

'*It was all about tapes, back then*' – Darryl McDaniels

If I could navigate the fuzz of traffic
reports, dinner table jazz and topical chat
*Majik FM!* is where, in the stillness between
last bell and the latch announcing mum's

3

return to dishes littering the kitchen sink,
I'd rest the red dial of the Sanyo cassette player
bought, part-exchange, from a now-defunct branch
of Tandy on Wandsworth High Street. Hours lost
to the underwear section of Littlewoods catalogue
gave way to R&B on E numbers, hi-hats the hiss
of hydraulic pistons, snares like tins dropped
on tiled floors. All of it piped in from back room studios,
sheds, distant kitchens haunted by teenage DJs hunched
over decks set up next to microwaves or, in pride of place,
on a good table usually reserved for special occasions.

We loved the casual bravado of emcees
with forty-a-day voices and too many ladies
to big up from last week's rave; years out of reach
but ours to keep on a TDK cassette, four in a pack,
for a pound. Most days I couldn't stretch,
pocket money spent on pick 'n' mix,
I'd plunder my mum's cache of cassettes
for something she wouldn't miss
or couldn't bring herself to admit
she once loved. Lucky Dube and Prince
were off limits. Kenny Rogers became
slick lyrics I could earn stripes by reciting
tomorrow lunch in front of anyone who'd listen,
if I could cut just the right amount of Sellotape,
make small enough balls of tissue to cover
the notches along the apex of each cassette.

Remember the days before your Walkman
was banished to a life in the attic?
How you cherished it, cutting a hole
in the lining of your blazer so you could

slip the silver box into the gap between the fabric,
pass an earpiece up one sleeve, rest your head
on one hand during maths class and ignore the talk
of vertices, indices, factorials, Napier Bones,
as you mouthed the lyrics,
brow crimped in concentration?

Soon, I'd used up all the dregs in mum's collection
and nothing was left save a black TDK, unmarked,
without a case. Thinking that it must be something
so laughable she couldn't bring herself to label,
I lifted it, weighed it in my hand, slid it cleanly
into place, pressed the play button and waited.

III.

My name rendered in a kettle-drum pitch
I knew to be my father's voice from the slight
twang of a lost tongue. *How old are you?*
I knew the boy's answer though I heard
only the hiss of static. *No, you're lying,*
*you are four years old.* If I was still a man
of faith I'd say he sat next to me that day
as I rewound the tape and asked me again
and again till streetlights bloomed through the still-
open curtains and settled in the lacquer of the table.

I started saving the odd pound coin here and there,
buying cassettes in bulk so I could record emcees,
study their lyrics, and pass off their bars as mine
moving from *yes, miss* to *Boom like TNT/the explosive*
*commentary/there is no similarity/to my originality*
in the time it took the teacher on duty to round the corner

and the regulars to form a rag-tag circle. I had a following;
girls two years older asking my name and *could you do
the one about the cartoon characters again?* Assemblies,
talent shows, tours of local junior schools, and lunchtimes
in the music room making haphazard recordings onto TDK
cassettes, broken tabs Sellotaped, a surfeit of fame secure.

Centre-stage, the keys dangling on a lanyard round my neck
were the jangling links of a gold chain; my budget shoes
doeskin loafers. Since I could spit lyrics every stone
thrown by those two boys, whose cries of *nig nog*
still follow me, bounced off my back; fell reverent at my feet.

At night, after mum snuffed the light, I'd practise,
under my breath, in bed; ape the latest tape
down to the last *big up ya chest* sliding from
*sum ah dem ah ay sum ah dem ah love dis* to
*in the venue we send you our menu that's the combo
emcee/dynamical lyrical tech emcee/I like it like the K-I-E.*
Soon I had my own chats. I was:

> *k to the a to the y to the o,*
> *lyrical G with a badboy flow*
> *if you don't know better get to know*
> *I'm k to the a to the y to the –*

Eminem ruined everything. I had to learn the words to 'Stan',
borrow the nasal whine, slide into a drawl midway between
London and New York and nowhere near Detroit.
In time, I could rattle off *The Slim Shady LP* line for line,
though no amount of practise could conjure the pale skin
and blue eyes that made Marshall *a poet* and me
just another brother who could rhyme.

# Fisherman's Song

What sadness for a fisherman
to navigate the blue
     and find among receding nets
strange, underwater blooms
     that look, at first, like bladderwrack
but from a closer view
     are clumps of matted human hair
atop an acrid soup.

And what song shall this fisherman
who loves a jaunty tune
     sing to lullaby his children
when dark shapes in their room
     make the night a snarling monster
only father's voice can soothe
     and who will soothe the fisherman
who navigates the blue?

# Broomhall

In light of what my aunt calls
the Arabic texture of my hair,
I'm Abdi outside the only shop
selling tamarind balls, Irish Moss,
Supermalt in decent quantities.

It is not enough to say I miss
the smell of cassava roasted
over open coals, expeditions
in want of tilapia, kapenta,
assorted meats of questionable

provenance. *How much, auntie?*
Barter and bluff and rough hands
of stallholders glazed to a deep
blue shameless blackness that is
consigned now to another life

before this one of middle-class
white boys in reggae bands, who
love roots and culture as if their
love is enough to know the code
that some of us live and die by.

At least these boys who call me
Abdi seem to be fond of Abdi.
They ask why I don't come
round no more, what it's like
in Leeds and maybe, today,
I can be Abdi and this shop
can be all the home I need.

# Winter Song

2002. Rapsz, Haystee, Kaystar,
JD, Sickness, Ashley and me
standing in the cold outside
Smokesta's house – Smokesta
is the only one we know who
owns a copy of Snowman,
Wiley Kat's latest white label.

I remember this as my bus
goes past what was once The Matapan,
now dubbed The Beacon Tree to rid
itself of infamy; this being the same spot
where Charles Butler was chased
round his car by a gunman, shot,
and collapsed in the road.

The songs we wanted to hear
lived on tapes of pirate radio sets
or in the first-hand crackle of vinyl
from Boogie Times or Rhythm Division.
When Snowman starts up, I'm back there,
in the arctic north of boyhood, lost
in the moment just before the bass drops.

# Guide to Proper Mixtape Assembly

The silence between songs can't be modulated by anything other than held breath. You have to sit and wait, time the release of the pause button to the last tenth of a second so that the gap between each track is a smooth purr, a TDK or Memorex your masterwork. Don't talk to me about your MP3 player how, given the limitless choice, you hardly ever listen to one song for more than two minutes at a time. Do you know about stealing double As from the TV remote so you can listen to last night's clandestine effort on the walk to school? You say you love music. Have you suffered the loss of a cassette so gnarled by a tape deck's teeth it refuses to play the beat you've come to recognise by sound and not name? Have you carried that theme in your head these years in the faint hope you might know it when it finds you, in a far-flung café, as you stand to pay, frozen, and the barista has to ask if you're okay?

# The Room

*'When you sample you're not only picking up that sound, you're picking up the room it was recorded in'* – ODDISEE

For the purist, hung up on tracing a drum break
to its source, acquired in the few moments' grace

before the store clerk, thin voiced, announces closing time,
it's not just the drummer's slack grip, how the hook line

swings in the session singer's interpretation,
or the engineer's too-loud approximation

of the MacGyver theme tune, it's that hiss, the room
fetching itself from itself in hiccups and spools.

Though there's a knack in telling A-side from remix
from test press that never saw the light of day,

mere completists never learn a good song's secret;
air displaced in *that* room – the breath of acetate.

## Some Bright Elegance

For the screwfaced in good shoes that paper
the walls of dance halls, I have little patience.
I say dance, not to be seen but free, your feet
are made for better things. Feel the bitterness
in you lift as it did for a six-year-old Bojangles,
tapping a living out of Richmond beer gardens
to the delight of a crowd that wasn't lynching
today but laughing at the quickness of the kid.

Throw yourself into the thick, emerging pure
reduced to flesh and bone, nerve and sinew.
Your folded arms understand music. Imagine
a packed Savoy Ballroom and slide across
the dusty floor as your zoot-suited Twenties
self, the feather in your hat from an ostrich,
the swagger in your step from the ochre dust
of a West African village. Dance for the times

you've been stalked by store detectives
for a lady on a bus, for the look of disgust
on the face of a boy too young to understand
why he hates but only that he must. Dance
for Sammy, dead and penniless, and for the
thousands still scraping a buck as street-corner
hoofers who, though they dance for their food,
move as if it is only them and the drums, talking.

## calling a spade a spade

'*What is the subconscious process of healing? What does it take? Perhaps it is something like how old schoolers would say you heal from a snake bite: having to spit out the venom again and again until there is no more*' – SAUL WILLIAMS

## The N Word

I.

You sly devil. Lounging in a Pinter script
or pitched from a transit van's rolled-down window;
my shadow on this unlit road, though you've been
smuggled from polite conversation. So when
a friend of a friend has you poised on his lips
you are not what he means, no call for balled fist,
since he's only signifyin(g) on the sign;
making wine from the bad blood of history.
Think of how you came into my life that day,
of leaves strewn as I had never seen them strewn,
knocking me about the head with your dark hands.

II.

*'Pretty little lighty but I can get dark'* – 'Get Dark', MZ BRATT

You came back as rubber lips, pepper grains, blik
you're so black you're blik and how the word stuck to
our tongues eclipsing – or so we thought – all fear
that any moment anyone might notice
and we'd be deemed the wrong side of a night sky.
Lately you are a *pretty little lighty* who can
*get dark* because, even now, dark means street
which means beast which means leave now for Benfleet.
These days I can't watch a music video
online without you trolling in the comments,
dressed to kill in your new age binary clothes.

## Alterity

Our match maker, the only other *other*
kid in class, was my best friend after the urge
passed to slap your negritude out of his mouth.
Knowing what it was to have the spotlight
we stood in line for auditions in the hall.
In lieu of a third we were the two magi,
honouring a blue-eyed plastic messiah,
bearing our gifts of thrifty chinoiserie.
The holy mother was a girl named Phyllis.
I had my words down three weeks before the show:
*Come, Melchior; let's make the best of the light.*

## The Cricket Test

Picture a cricket match, first week at upper
school, blacks versus whites, that slight hesitation
on choosing a side, and you're close to knowing
why I've been trying to master this language.
Raised as I was, some words in this argot catch
in the throat, seemingly made for someone else
(the sticking point from which all else is fixed).
We lost to a one-handed catch. After the match
our changing room was a shrine to apartheid.
When I crossed the threshold, Danny asked me why
I'd stand here when I could be there, with my kind.

## The Conservatoire System

All of that to fetch up here, on secondment
to the institute of whiteface minstrelsy –
where I must flay myself nightly or risk
the indignity of being seen, in blackness,
*as I am* or as I've been taught, from without,
I am; an unconvincing Everyman.
But why would I want to be that dry bastard
with his pronouncements on all that can be seen
and practice this, his art of self-effacement, by which
he shakes off the vulgarity of being,
the better to make himself praiseworthy?

## On Reading 'Colloquy in Black Rock'

Just when I think I've shaken you off, you're there,
innocuous, in Lowell's poem – a flag
out of fashion, still flown by a patriot.
The seminar tutor tiptoes round you now.
Ours is to note the working mind behind the word
not what remains unsaid: there is *us* and *them*.
Cut to requisite dreads, beads, a wooden pendant
in the shape of a home I can't remember,
*The Autobiography of Malcolm X.*
Our first time alone together she asks
me why no one in my pictures is white.

## Varsity Blues

an all-white production of *for colored girls...*
I expect my lecturer to get the joke
but he's credulous, the theatrical risk
becoming, in his mind, a piece in *The Stage*:
*Drama student critiques our post-race moment.*
I cast a banker's daughter from the second year
as the Lady in Blue in spite of the minstrel-
show tone she affects to suggest otherness.
A student reporter praises the vision
of the production, the authenticity
of the performances, the light and shade.

## Casting

My agent says I have to use my street voice.
Though my talent is for rakes and fops I'll drop
the necessary octaves, stifle a laugh
at the playwright's misplaced *get me blud* and *safe*.
If I get it they'll ask how long it takes me
to grow *cornrows* without the small screen's knowing
wink. Three years RADA, two years rep and I'm sick
of playing *lean dark men who may have guns.*
I have a book of poems in my rucksack,
blank pad, two pens, tattered A-Z, headphones
that know Prokofiev as well as Prince Paul.

## Callbacks

I have to stop working on my one-man show
to take the call. They liked me, but *could I try*
*being Riley*, sotto voce, *the blind negro?*
When I got signed, my agent told me *never*
*say no to good money.* She left out the part
about playing Sam in every room, itching,
of course, to play a tune. I take it (rent's due).
Besides, I would like to divide critical
opinion just once. I'll play him well-spoken.
My agent is elated. That's great, she says,
*you're perfect for this role, you were born to play it.*

## Normative Ethics

In the safe distance of objectivity,
you can speak, with a straight face, of being
*on the margins*, being thought no longer *cool*
(if you don't know the curse that coolness confers):
women who prize your *chocolate voice* above
your words, or look at you like you've deserted
*the cause* because you are holding hands with your
*Muzungu*. Men who tut like you've stolen
their birthright. A colleague, who doesn't see you,
angry at her own half-blackness, who *can't*
*believe* her best friend is *fucking a nigger*.

# Curfew

*This was soldier curfew* he says, apropos
of nothing, the way the best stories come
round this table that just about holds us,

bwali all but eaten, the flash of the thought
a flame lighting up his face. He rests the tip
of a finger in the space between his eyes,

*past curfew there were no warning shots.*
Auntie chips in as if this were little more
than a scene they were rehearsing: *you had*

*to have a man with you at all times, especially*
*at night, so my cousin would walk me home.*
*In trousers and squared shoulders she could pass.*

She smiles a knowing smile at our scandalised
faces. Faces we've bent into anguished shapes
when she could smell a lie but let us improvise

wildly until, hoist by our respective petards,
we came clean, deferring to the knowledge
of a woman who was a girl who could climb

out of a window in hotpants and platforms,
dance to the last ache in her legs and make
it back before the cockerel crowed morning.

# 25 October, 1964

*'Recently, a very close friend of mine declared it would take us another twenty years to be really independent. Was he right? I am afraid there is a lot of truth in this'* – DR. KENNETH KAUNDA, 1966

We danced like Celts the day the news of it
kicked the District Commissioner's fat rump.
Teachers who beat us till we couldn't sit
over little things, were, by lunch, so drunk
Mr Chishala shut the school and followed
his staff to a bar where colonial notes
came back as loose change, baked groundnuts, hallowed
pitchers of the local brew (a throat song
known as Mosi). They drank to the freedom
our children would inherit, then raised a glass
to Leyland's Hippo-shaped buses, heaving
with the copper belt's weary underclass
who, in spite of a new nation, were still dressed
in hunched shoulders, the shame of unpuffed chests.

# Legerdemain

and, at last, you have come upon
the jewel in the crown of our collection
here at the Royal Museum for Central Africa:
a magnifying glass used by one
of the King's functionaries
who, by Royal decree, remained
unsung among the sons of Europe
until recently. Note the engraving
on the ivory handle that tells us
this glass was used in the Kasai.
Since the official report was redacted
some of you might be unaware
of this particular brand of magic:
the 'trick was to use a magnifying
glass to light a cigar, "after which
the white man explained his intimate
relation to the sun, and declared
that if he were to request [the sun]
to burn up his black brother's
village it would be done"'–
and so it was the land changed hands
as a cigar, given light, becomes a stub
and its smoke that stays with you
is the smoke from a burning village.

# How to Build Cathedrals

*after Cildo Meireles*


To think, when the Cessna's
wheels bumped the makeshift

runway, women-folk walked
uncovered and the men knew

nothing of their godly duties.
I started them on the Gospels.

Marianne instilled the finer points
of feminine deportment. Before long

they knew the principal scriptures
by heart and could recite the Hail Mary

in the perfect broken English
our predecessors bequeathed them.

We've had a number of successes:
children wake afraid of God's wrath,

ladies wear brassieres and the gents
cease gambling on the Sabbath day.

In the last sermon before hurricane season
I say, tapping my breast, *this* is a church.

Waves

The year waves came in, when we sang
*you're sweet like chocolate, boy*
without shame, everyone had a method

for taming even the most rebellious head
of pepper grains into slick, crazy-paved,
deference to R&B stars looming large

from hoardings, pasted into diaries
and exercise books, their lyrics written
out on the backs of hands. We wanted

to be wanted like that, so we slept with
our mothers' head wraps tight, to keep
the facade in place. Some taught themselves

the grace of clippers, so they could tidy
up their edges in the bathroom mirror,
others sought the counsel of barbers,

technicians of the razor blade
who could elevate a trim to a thing
of head-turning, transcendent beauty.

But for all we tried to hide our stubble,
ashamed of the hair's natural grain,
it came back unbidden as if each follicle

knew that soon we would covet shaved
lines in sideburns, eyebrows, anything
to set ourselves apart, betray our roots.

# Malumbo

*for Malaika*

Your parents rejected my suggestion.
I told them you could pull off *Ethel*.
The jury is still out, *Alesha* out of the question
(ditto *Shaniqua* and *Chantelle*).
I've a soft spot for *Dambisa*, *Malaika*, or *Mambwe*
but, whatever you are called, you should know
we've all been waiting for your birthday;
the look on your face as you apprehend snow.
I hope you hold on to your wonder
that you'll never grow so stiffly poised
a scent or song is not enough to conjure
that smile of yours, the fullness of your voice.

# Orientation

Buy yourself a copy of *Labyrinths* by Jorge Luis Borges. Turn to page 83. Read the fourteenth sentence aloud. Speaking these words will cause a set of coordinates to be burned into the skin of your left forearm. Follow them till you reach a war monument where you will see a man in a homemade lobster costume. Ask him if he has any suppositories. Let him guide you to a quiet spot where he'll produce an apple strudel which you should eat. Outside a '67 Pontiac Firebird will wait. Take the driver's seat by force. Under the seat you'll find a sheaf of papers. On these papers will be written in a script only you can decipher, your original name.

# How to Cry

I'm going to fold, as an overloaded trestle folds,
in the middle of Romford Market and bawl
the way my small niece bawls for her mother
when she leaves the room. In spite
of our assurances, already the little one knows
that those who leave might never come back.

Though I keep God in a small closed box
I'll prostrate myself outside Argos,
beat the cobbles with my palm
till blood rings in my fingertips. There, amid
cockneys selling fish, *box-fresh from Billingsgate*,
tears will occur to eyes I thought I'd cried out.

I want to be set off by our red brick uni,
its array of strange faces. Show me round
the flat that stinks of our sleeplessness,
plans hatched in the whispers of small hours.
I'm tired of this strength. Let me be bereft,
watching the white limousine as it drives away.

# Loch Long by Ardgartan, Argyll

Where night is a crow
troubling the surface of the water
and the light of morning
is the breadth of a lover's gaze
and the loch-side mist
gives you back to landscape
I'll wait for you.

Where headlights are slow fish
swimming miles of cobbled river
and this cigarette's glow
is the effortless grace of a firefly
and your troubles are bright
as paper lanterns given to the sky
by fire, you'll find me.

Where the ends of the earth
are the view from a cabin window
and the past is an old song
nobody knows how to sing anymore
and this moment is sudden rain
soaking you through to the skin
I'll meet you.

# Kumukanda

Since I haven't danced among my fellow initiates,
following a looped procession from woods at the edge
of a village, Tata's people would think me unfinished –
a child who never sloughed off the childish estate
to cross the river boys of our tribe must cross
in order to die and come back grown.

I was raised in a strange land, by small increments:
when I bathed my mother the days she was too weak,
when auntie broke the news and I chose a yellow suit
and white shoes to dress my mother's body,
at the grave-side when the man I almost grew to call
dad, though we both needed a hug, shook my hand.

If my alternate self, who never left, could see me
what would he make of these literary pretensions,
this need to speak with a tongue that isn't mine?
Would he be strange to me as I to him, frowning
as he greets me in the language of my father
and my father's father and my father's father's father?

# H-O-R-S-E

August. Each of us in shorts, a white tee.
This warmth has brought the ballers out in force.

And though he's been dead since 1993
my father and I play a game of H-O-R-S-E.

Next to us, a group of friends play three on three
backed by Biggie's elegant contortions

(to better demonstrate the importance
of style). I stop, push off from my right knee

willing the flick of my wrist to yield the sort
of gorgeous arc that's talked about for weeks.

The rim gives back the sound of falling short.
I pass the ball to the top of the key.

Tata throws up a fade-away and scores.
I can't match him, and collect the letter 'e'.

# Alternate Take

When they laid our father out, mwaice wandi,
I want to say – I'm meant to say – soft light
played the skin of his spent face and the sobs
were, of course, a jangling kind of song.

If I could take you where the sandy earth
meets his final stone, tiled and off-white,
we might have learned to worship better gods.
He was known, in the shebeens, as *long John*.

At the wake relatives tried variations
on the words of the day: *I am sorry*
*for your grieving/your trouble/your loss.*
I've been weighing these apologies for years

that pass and retreat like disused stations.
I think of his walk becoming your quarry,
his knack for beguiling women, your cross.
It's enough to bring me here, past tears

to where his face simplifies to a picture:
the shrine in Nagoya, him stood, sequoia
among lesser trees, looking good in denim;
every inch the charismatic spectre.

In his memory my voice bears his tincture –
saxophone played low / boy raised on soya
porridge, chloroquine, a promise of heaven.
There are days I think I'm only a vector

carrying him slowly to my own graveyard,
and standing at the lectern, rather than my son,
will be another copy: the same sharp
edge to the chin, that *basso profundo* hum.

Kid brother, we breathers have made an art
of negation, see how a buckled drum
is made from a man's beating heart
and a fixed gaze is a loaded weapon.

# A Proud Blemish

The year I graduate from size eights,
learn to walk in the grown man's shoes
contradicting the diminutive frame
I parade across the Arndale estate:

2step is an airborne sickness, infecting
every discerning cassette deck,
after-hours wine bar, joy rider's car.
Most weekends I try to fool a woman

accustomed to the lies of men, sneak home
an hour shy of her footfall in the hallway,
to rehearse my lines: *I was home... I just
...didn't hear the phone*, the beep

of the answering machine, her repeating
my name till it's a prayer, voice two parts
ire, one despair, that her days are riven
between shift patterns and her only son.

By the time I graduate size nines, understand
*Caesarean* when she answers my question:
*did it hurt?* Shows me the dark groove hidden
under her work shirt, a proud blemish in skin

rippled with ridges from weight loss. She knows
it's not stress. We sit, lumps in throats,
wait on tests. *They don't know what's wrong*
she says, next day she's back to underground

tunnels, thousands riding the same choppy waves.
Soon she's too weak to walk or wash herself.
The bones of her skull vitiate a face that once
stunned grown men into mumbling stupors.

On a grey ward, two months in to size elevens,
she speaks in my mother tongue, begs me trace
the steps of its music, but the discord of two
languages keeps me from the truth I won't hear.

She's dying but I won't call her dead, can't let mum
become a body, a stone, an empty hospital bed.

# Orphan Song

When night is at its ripeness
I think of the songs they'll play
at my funeral. For all I know death
is like watching a landscape dissolve
through the window of an overheating
coach, bound for the nearest airport.

And if passing out of this life
is like passing through check-in
to be felt up by surly officials,
being carried aloft in a wooden box
must be like pushing back on a runway;
entering the next life like landing.

Who will greet me when I alight?
Will my parents be standing there,
reconciled, glancing at their watches,
with Kenta, rid of his jaundiced glow,
and the twins, grown to their full height?

# Grief

What became of the boy
who called himself Grief?
The boy who, the story ran,
harboured a gun
through the back-roads
and alleyways of his teens,
the boy who turned up
as a footnote the night
we played *my ends are rougher than your ends*
in a flat overlooking London Road –
frontline of a post-code war
so far removed
we chuckled when someone said
kebabs from the shop that wore
a fresh batch of memorial flowers
were *to die for.*
Grief was grit
to lend the fable texture.
We never knew the name
his mum called him,
or what reduced him to plying
the night trade so white kids
could say they *bun high grade.*
He is a boy caught between commas
in a news report about youth crime,
an image fixed in place
by someone else's language.

# The Nod

When we're strangers that pass each other
in the street, it will come down to this tilt
of the head – acknowledging another
version of events set in a new-build
years from now, a mess of a place filled
with books and records, our kids thick as thieves
redefining all notions of mischief.

Perhaps our paths will cross in a city
of seven hills as the light draws your face
out from the bliss of anonymity.
Maybe you'll be stroking the goose-down nape
of a small child with eyes the exact shade
of those I met across a room at the start
of this pain-in-the-heart, this febrile dance.

# In Defence of Darkness

Drum-brush of fabric. The clink of a zip
on laminate floor. You step from a skirt
to the sound of the street outside swelling
with traffic, the sound of our breathing.

We've time to touch like we used to –
the harshness of the journey written
into the depth of a clinch. Chest to chest,
your head in the cleft of my breastbone.

Coconut oil, laundry detergent, sweat,
dry shampoo, Burberry Weekend.
Garam masala tang in the troublesome
hair inherited by our possible daughter.
I kneel, the better to drown in your scent.

Since I'm remembering this, or making it up,
there is only darkness; our bodies speaking.
*Eat*, you ask. I eat – savouring
your aftertaste: tart but sweet, the inside
of a cheek, cured meat, a local delicacy.

# Andrews Corner

### I.

Where an old man comes, to practise
standing still, tutting
that the street he fought to keep is gone
and, sixty years on, he doesn't belong
to this world of bass, blasting out of
passing cars, and earshot, at the speed
of an age when pubs close down
overnight; are mounds of rubble in a week.

### II.

Where flowers moulder in memory of Tash,
fifteen, her twenty-something boyfriend
too drunk to swerve and miss the tree,
girls own their grown woman outfits,
smile at boys who smell of weed and too much
CK One. Pel, who can get served, stands in line.
Outside his friends play the transatlantic
dozens; the correct answer is always your mum.

### III.

Where alleys wake to condom wrappers,
kebab meat, a ballet pump, last week
a van pulled up and it was blood. Today:
joggers dodge a dead pigeon, offer wordless
greeting to the night bus's army of sanguine-
eyed ravers, nursing bad skin and tinnitus.
Goaded by the light, past the same house on repeat,
they think of taking off their shoes; inviolable sleep.

# Martins Corner

Meat wagons sing an ode in sardonics
passing a bus held briefly to regulate

the service. *Jesus loves you*, if you
believe in signage. High heels clack,

are slung off, taken in hand. A shawl
flicked around our lady's shoulders

flutters. She speeds up by Londis
past friends pressed against shutters

huddled, from the cold, round a zoot
two-sed then snuffed by a scuffed shoe.

This is the hour when a silver glimpse,
likely a phone, is a blade and a patch

of shade must be an assailant. A couple
on their second date claim a requisite

slow-dance in the space where restraint
cuts its eye at recklessness, their arms

charm necklaces warding off the thought
of these limbs round some other necks;

the night, years hence, when they'll forget
how to want and need in the same breath.

## Kung'anda

The English newsreader told me
home was a broken man, holding
a dying child, with flies round its mouth:

a story that didn't tally with my mother's,
of childhood smiles on granddad's farm
or the laughing dance across hot soil

to the ice-cream stand. No tagline
could capture the air, swelling
with moisture after dry season

or the glistening brown torsos
of children bathed in the promise
of rainclouds, kept at last.

# 'Round Midnight

Hour of bones singing a blues of cold
setting in, camp beds, vouchsafed mattresses
in overcrowded rooms. The lost growing old

in post-industrial towns, words in their heads
from the tongues of long-defunct countries
and only these words in case they forget

where they were born, street names, all those sundries
that, in retrospect, amount to a life.
Who stops to take note of the smell of trees

this leave-taking hour, turning like Edith
to commit a burning place to memory,
knowing, even in this harshest of lights,

what's unrecorded is a reverie
faded in a year, gone in a century?

## Baltic Mill

Though you maintain the elements
have conspired against us we still
inch the cobbled street past Castle
Keep down to the Quayside's rain-
slick paving slabs all for the thrill
of standing across from Baltic Mill
in a turbid mist lifted from the Tyne.

We planned to catch a talk at the Laing
or the Biscuit but, pushed for time,
plumped for a backstreet pizzeria, throw-
back to another world, a haberdasher's
maybe or greasy spoon for blackface
minstrels from Gateshead mines and
iron works. The North Sea wind-chill

bids us leave behind this city of faces
cast in stories passed down, vestige
of years when hundreds of miles stood
between us. The exact course that brought
us here is unimportant. It is that we met
like this river, drawn from two sources,
offered up our flaws, our sedimental selves.

# This poem contains gull song

not song, as such, so much
as guttural injunction; a music
we forgot how to understand, since
it lacks that carefully planned sweetness
sounding instead of black-shod
clockers-on, the splash and clack
of shop fronts, cabbies sparking
tabs in the cold of a windswept rank
flanked by one of Monkchester's
lesser monuments; a sentry stopped
in his bronze tracks, steps echoing
the strains of an old tune hidden
in the genes of a new one – a left-behind
accent fizzing at the back of my tongue.

# For those orphaned late in life

What if the wind blowing through
the french doors of your childhood
is the house's way of saying goodbye
and when you call out, answering
yourself, greeting the gone out of habit,
you hear, for the first time, the timbre
of your voice how someone else might?

# Notes

'Self-Portrait as a Garage Emcee': the poem contains brief quotations from garage songs and freestyles: Nikki S and Nyke ('Boom like TNT...'), Craig David ('sum a dem a ay sum a dem a luv dis...'), and Godsgift ('in the venue we send you our menu...'). 'Enter with the Eastender...' is a folk lyric of unknown provenance (the names mentioned are characters from a popular UK TV programme), '[I'm] k to the a to the y to the o ...' is the author's riff on a rhyme that was common in UK garage circa 2000.

'Broomhall': kapenta are a kind of small fish.

'Some Bright Elegance': the poem's title is taken from a passage in Amiri Baraka's poem, 'The Dance': 'and all his words ran out of it: that there / was some bright elegance the sad meat / of the body made'.

'Casting': contains a line from Clare Pollard's poem, 'The Panther'.

'Legerdemain': the poem contains material from George Washington Williams's open letter to King Leopold II, as quoted in *King Leopold's Ghost* by Adam Hochschild.

'H-O-R-S-E': A basketball training exercise. The object of the game is to score a basket so skilful that your opponent cannot replicate it. Each time an opponent fails to replicate their counterpart's successful shot they receive a letter from the word 'horse'.

'Alternate Take': 'mwaice wandi' is a Bemba endearment equivalent to the phrase kid brother or sister.

'Kung'anda': is a Bemba word meaning home.

''Round Midnight': Edith is thought to have been the name of Lot's Wife.

'This poem contains gull song': Monkchester is one of the old names of Newcastle upon Tyne.

# Acknowledgements

I would like to thank the editors of the following publications in which some of these poems first appeared: *Ambit, Magma, Out of Bounds* (Bloodaxe, 2011), *Ploughshares, Poetry International Web, Poetry London, The Poetry Review, The Salt Book of Younger Poets* (Salt, 2012), *The Best British Poetry* (Salt, 2011, 2013, 2015), *The World Record* (Bloodaxe, 2012) and *Ten: The New Wave* (Bloodaxe, 2014).

Several of these poems were also published in two pamphlets, *Some Bright Elegance* (Salt, 2012) and *The Colour of James Brown's Scream* (Akashic, 2016).

'Self-Portrait as a Garage Emcee' was commissioned by Apples and Snakes for *The Word's A Stage* and performed at The Soho Theatre.

An extract from 'calling a spade a spade' was awarded the 2012 Geoffrey Dearmer Prize (judged by Jane Draycott).

'Loch Long by Ardgartan, Argyll' was commissioned by Apples and Snakes and RIBA in response to a photographic exhibition featuring the work of Edwin Smith. 'This poem contains gull song' was written as part of the Bloodaxe Archive project, a collaboration between Bloodaxe, Newcastle Centre for Literary Arts, and The Poetry School.

'Winter Song' was commissioned by BBC Radio 4 and broadcast on Front Row, 21 December 2016.

This collection was begun in earnest as part of a residency at Cove Park in 2013.

Thanks also to: Parisa Ebrahimi, Jolyon Roberts, Joelle Taylor, Monika Neall, Dorothea Smartt, Skorpio Da Nemesis (R.I.P), BREIS, Charlie Dark, Jacob Sam-La Rose, Roger Robinson, Zena Edwards, Niall O'Sullivan, Poetry Society, Apples and Snakes, Spread The Word, all my Sheffield people (especially the 225 Crookesmoor Road, 423 Glossop Road, and Tuesday Club extended family), Les Robinson, Roddy Lumsden, Bernardine Evaristo, Nathalie Teitler, Anthony Joseph, Sean Graham, all Complete Works fellows, Anna Kirk, Rachel Piercey, James Trevelyan, Jay Bernard, Inua Ellams, Yemisi Turner-Blake, Warsan Shire, Jasmine Cooray, Miriam Nash, Sarah Perry, Monika Navarro, Rowena Knight, Mum and Dad (R.I.P), The Kaulu, Chingonyi, Siameja and Yonga families, Auntie Florence, Uncle Kenneth, Kaimba, Sempela, Chilufya, Katai, Yande, Louise, Adina, and Malaika.